Aurora Cantus

Aurora Cantus

A Poet's Book of Hours

Aurora Cantus

A Poet's Book of Hours

Silvia Passiflora

Scriptaluna Press

Aurora Cantus: A Poet's Book of Hours
Copyright © 2026 Scriptaluna
Edited by Amanda Dzimianski

For information address:
Scriptaluna LLC
1270 Caroline Street, D120 #110
Atlanta, GA 30307

First edition

Cover design by Silvia Passiflora
Typeset by Silvia Passiflora

ISBN 979-8-9959704-0-8
Library of Congress Control Number 2026913755

Set in Caladea · Printed in the United States of America

To the eagles and the doves —
who found me when I was alone, and stayed

Aurora Cantus
dawn's golden songs beckon me
singing light prayers

Aurora Cantus: A Poet's Book of Hours

Dawn: At First Hours

Noon: The Disappearing Quiet

Aurora Cantus: A Poet's Book of Hours

Between: Still Hours

Again: The Open Field

Introduction

In the thirteenth century, books of hours became some of the most familiar, intimate books in Europe. These private, devotional manuscripts contained prayers, psalms, calendars, and sacred readings arranged around the hours of the day. Often commissioned by women and carried into marriages that sealed alliances across borders, these books passed through generations and into the margins of daily life. From the thirteenth to the seventeenth centuries, if a household owned a single book, it was this one.

Because they were commissioned by women, these books depicted the Virgin Mary as a reader, seated at her desk as the angel Gabriel arrived to announce the conception of the Christ child. Luke's Gospel makes no such claim. Still, the image endured. Mary with a book open before her became one of the most painted scenes in Western art. A woman holding the book of hours was invited to recognize herself there.

These books were written in the vernacular rather than the Latin of the educated class, from which women were largely excluded. Scripture entered the language of daily life, and something quiet began to shift.

These poems were written in the same spirit — in the exhausted hours between systems and silence, between deadlines and waiting. I returned to them the way others once returned to a book of hours: trying to keep faith with the day.

Aurora Cantus is Latin for "dawn song" — the music of first light. I named this collection for the hours in which it was written: late at night, before sunrise, at kitchen tables, in the changing light of ordinary days. My publishing press, Scriptaluna, means "writing under the moon."

From the Threshold

Between July and November 2025, I submitted two albums and a single for Grammy® consideration. During those months, I wrote more than three hundred poems. The submission process itself was strangely invisible. The portal opened in July. The nominations would not be announced until November. In between stretched a season of uncertainty, technical systems, and waiting. I reached out for help wherever I could find it. Some doors closed gently. Others opened.

What held me through that season was the poems. Writing became the only place where the grief and confusion of those months could take their full shape without interruption.

The eagle poems in this collection are for those who arrived beside me when the crossing narrowed. The rest became the record of what it costs.

— Silvia Passiflora

Dawn: At First Hours

July 17 – July 28, 2025

Dawn Song

The world still blinks against the light
before the naming of all things

Its soul remembers open hills
where spider silk catches wind

The hush before the kettle sings
before the sparrow splits the sky

before any of earth's trembling —
wiping dew from morning's eye

I wake still wrapped inside the veil
and reach for what the dark made plain

dawn songs flow without judgment
I give them all a name

Before the Earth Remembers Noise

The earth is not asleep, no
it crackles soft like infant flame
a thrush-song warbling in its throat
waiting to turn the page

Each bloodroot receives its private tone
a tuning fork of sap and skin
even the worms beneath the stones
begin to hum the day within

No bell has rung, no hand has prayed
but still the veil begins to thin
like an orchestra inhaling
the first notes begin to spin

Sunward

I turned my face toward morning's blaze
the vaults behind me cold with moss
I sing alive to weathered angels
with breath and borrowed psalms

The strings I pluck are made of light
drawn from the marrow of the breeze
and every chord I press to sing
unfastens silence from the trees

I'm not family to those who rest
whose legacies hum in granite rows
but came to pay respects
to these names I do not know

Tea Leaves Brewing

In china cups, fragrant tea is poured
hibiscus blooms in tropic hues
while passionfruit's sweetness I adore
gentle steam stirs the air anew

I settle down on a Southern porch
no longer calling out to those who pass
wrens tuck softly above the door
clay dusk-light breathing out at last

Line by line, his words arrived —
the poet of the mountains
and I, answered back in kind
from the Southern gardens

The leaves below my cup lie open
markings shifting as they dry —
I do not name what's forming yet
but the patterns begin to signal

Noon: The Disappearing Quiet

July 29 — August 4, 2025

The Canary in the Distance

I asked the world to care
I offered them music, poems, witness
the numbers said they saw it
while the silence deepened

Some scroll past the art
the way they scroll past headlines
not out of cruelty
just habits of exhaustion

Sometimes I wonder
if we cannot hear the song
carried carefully toward them
how will we hear

the canary in the distance?

Sleep Tastes of Salt

Last night the sheets were damp with tears
the room too loud with clocks I could not shush
each hour passed, a dance, a minuet of fears
in clumsy steps of one

I write at the dead of night, post at midnight
the numbers look away
the lurkers sleep or say nothing
the moon at least will stay

Yet morning found me standing all the same
my sheets still warm from battles in the bed
I dressed my wounds and did not speak their name
I made the coffee — I was not yct dead

For Those Who Troll

I poured it out in public
the whole long year paid with grit and skin
a few answered back with emojis
the lone reply: *awards don't mean anything*

I stopped going to your shows
even though you were next door
there will be no dramatic goodbye notes or empty tears
the note in blue simply reads: I left
an hour ago

Between the Plow and Mule

By August, the planting turned toward winter
my hands forget the lines they traced
the plow is dull and handles splintered
the sun is branded on my face

The fence is broken, held by a rock
the mule won't look me in the eye
I thought I had chosen well — then saw
the first planting had run dry

The rows are numbered now
but working them is not
six passes through the same hard ground
to plant what I forgot

And yet the wind still smells of peaches
there's lightning in my bones
these songs I write require keywords
in fields too small for what they hold

I thought each pass would be the last
until another absence rose
I sow the last lines carefully —
this time the rooting holds

Watching the Sky for Clouds to Break

The heron stands in music streams
one leg lifted like a compass
pointing with the old knowing
that minnows flicker only once

The persimmon does not blush in summer
she ripens after the heat
persevering through the season's turn
until her sweetness yields

And the Chess Queen
watching from the reeds
with eyes on every square
lets the knight tempt and the rook chase —
but when the cloud clears just enough
one move could end the game

The Narrow Crossing

I realized too late
the catalog had split its river twice —

one hand reaching for royalties
another already claiming the toll

So I took the albums down myself

Thirty days, the warning flashed
after I was already in the water —
but the portal was closing

Here? one platform
dark

Here? the ford —
transit blurred beneath the streaming

Here? I could not tell
I'll watch again tomorrow

I could not return the way I came
by then the debut was already sworn upon my hand
no safer going forward than turning back —
on the banks behind me
witnesses with hands covering their mouths

no label
no manager
no coachmen waiting at the gate
only the crossing and whatever courage remained

Each morning I searched the banks —
I gambled on the crossing
one title clearing,
while another disappeared beneath it

The Three Flights of the Dove

The raven never came back.
He liked the chaos,
the endless buffet of bones
on water's black mirror.

But I —
I was the one they trusted
with the first word of land.

The first time I flew,
the sky was still mourning,
the ocean still wearing the mountains
like a funeral shawl.
I came back
with nothing but wet feathers
and a question in my eyes.
They held me.
Let me rest.
Waited seven days,
as if time could change the tilt of the earth.

The second time
I found a single olive leaf,
trembling in the mouth of a broken tree.
I brought it back,
a prophecy between my beak.
They wept.

The third time.
The world had made room for me.
I chose to stay
with the promise of fruit.

Angels with the Flaming Swords

I met them barefoot at the gate
those warrior angels with blades of flame
their swords like lightning trapped in steel
their silence taut with holy blame

They asked for proof I bore the mark
I showed them scars from binding cords
metadata seared in my hands
my lips aflame, incanting words

They circled close, their wings ablaze
my own wings, feathered coal and gray
they smelled of frankincense and myrrh
I smelled of muscadine and clay

But when I roared with rage
for I had crossed too much dark water
to leave those watching from the shore

they saw the costly *yes* within

They laid their weapons at my feet
one touched my cheek and simply said:

"Ah… you are one of our own."

Between: Still Hours
August 5 — December 2025

Momentum Angelorum at 2:22

Wrapped in warm cloth,
like a letter not yet opened,
I sit still,
but something is moving.

Not the polish,
not the breath of lavender
but the angels —
soft-footed, circling.

They do not knock.
They do not instruct.
They hum in a language
that only comfort understands.

This is the momentum of mercy,
the lift that begins
with sitting down.

At 2:22,
they remind me:
even stillness has velocity
when it is chosen.

After the Return to Ithaca

At last, I dream beside my dogs
their paws twitch through sleep
chasing ghosts that haunt the forest moss
too travel-worn to weep

My bed, after all the returning, now holds me
like a lover who's forgiven everything
the judges have vanished, at least for tonight
only the moon remains, still whispering

Ulysses returned without trumpets
no microphones, just a dog who wept
so too I crawl home changed

praised elsewhere

Enough of Signs

The rocking chair did not move
until she did —
and even then, it asked
for permission.

After the hard birthing
of twin albums
that nearly bled her dry,
she wasn't waiting for a sign.

She'd had enough of signs.

In this moment,
all that mattered was the feeling
of being held and cradled.

The porch squeaked in accordance anyway —
like a fiddle settling
to a metronome,
like a village
that shows up
after the babies are born.

Portrait of the Morning: The Rosary Room

I.

Steam rises, entwined
the kitchen welcomes morning
coffee in mid-prayer

II.

Fingers trace the beads
like footsteps on old floorboards
each name, a small light

III.

Curtains do not move
only the sun makes a sound
whispering *amen*

Mother Sun

I stand at the threshold
barefoot in the yielding sky
leaning on the soft blue doorframe of the horizon

Inside, you are still wrapped in the blankets of night
breathing in the slow rhythm of dreams

I smooth the edges of the dark
so they will not snag when you rise
and lay a gold ribbon
across your floor to guide you

I do not wake you yet
I watch carefully instead
marveling at the faces you make in sleep
at the way your hands rest like tiny altars
and how your heart
is already lifting toward me

I wonder who you will become
and what glory awaits you
of your own making

When you open your eyes
I will already be here
warming the milk
singing you into the day

The Sound of One Hand Clapping

It is said
the sound of one hand clapping
is no sound at all

I think of those
who stood in the doorway
of my life
long enough to be seen
but not long enough to see

I whispered offerings on repeat
a flyer shared, a payment code taped up, a cake
a soft reminder:
I am here, I saw you

But no cake with candles came back
no echo
not even a breeze
from their passing

Creatures of Habit

The spider builds
the same web each morning
because the thread is already inside
no questions asked
no need to choose a different corner

The hermit crab
backs into safety
a borrowed shell
fitting over softness
called *home* out of habit

The sea turtle returns
to the original shore
even when the tide
bites deeper than memory
the digging begins anyway

The mockingbird lands
on the same fence post
though the sky is wide
repetition becomes
the song most known

And I
with limbs unbound
and voice uncautioned
still whisper old rules
as if they protect

Not all pattern is prison
but what we live without examining
shrinks the possible
until there was never a gate

Staunch the Bleeding After the Mountaintop

I bound my hands just tight enough to climb
the rope burned, but I ascended
the night would not close its eyes

Above the Blue Ridge tree line, the wind softened
I planted my flag with fingers torn open
thinking the summit was the view

It was never the mountain that broke me
it was the bargain
the way I bartered future fruit
the price paid in flesh for higher ground

Now I dress the wound myself

Wrap the bone before it splits again
no more tribute to spectators
who never carried
weight

There's a war in my blood
and another at the gate
yet sleep will not take me

The Hummingbird Cake

She doesn't open the oven.
Not yet.
The air is still full
of banana and prayer,
cinnamon and careful breath.

She walks away,
then walks back.
Waiting,
like waiting for word from a friend
who said they'd call
when they could.

The pecans remember last summer.
The pineapple holds the secret.
The eggs know something
about binding what was broken.

She turns the light on
but does not open the door.
Even love needs heat
before it rises.

Shoes in Hand

The traveler rose before dawn
the village still curled in sleep

She heard old grudges clucking
like hens in schoolyard teams
and horses neighing through the fence:

"Who does she think she is?"

But their eyes had never wandered
past the hills beyond the pond

She knew her heart was not meant
to echo such small sounds

With shoes in hand
she tiptoed past the brackish water,
the dog yapping at the gate

Behind her,
the village vanished into fog

The First Eagle
(for Tamanie)

I was circling too low
talons full of my own snare
vision blurred by the dust I'd kicked up

Then she came
with broad wings steady
eyes gold as sunrise on stone

I flew this path, she said
just now, for another
and turned mid-flight to show me
here, the current —
here, the cliff —
here, where the air holds

And she stayed
until I felt my pulse slow
and my wings remembered
what they were for

The Second Eagle
(for Daniel)

From the ridge where the first eagle left her
she watched the valley churn
the baton cooling in her grip

She had flown this far on instinct
turned away from every ridge
one field from the finish line

But from the far horizon
came the shadow of another eagle
slicing the sky without strain
carrying the scent of familiar winds

He crossed beside her
wingtip near enough
for the air between them
to change

You were made for this air

Together we rode the updraft
beyond the last known ridge

September Bones

The sourwoods had begun loosening
their red signatures into the yard
each leaf a small surrender

For weeks I had lived by glowing windows
names flickering across midnight screens
crossing the dark like migrating geese
toward beacons already lit

A warmth settled into the body afterward
the kind that comes
when the climb is over for now
and campfires appear along the ridge

The mornings cooled at last
I walked slower through the neighborhood
hands deep in my sleeves
breathing woodsmoke and thawed rain

I had already heard
other wings in the distance
answering back

Somewhere beyond the season's turning
ballots drifted through invisible rooms
the trees releasing what they could
into the hands of the wind

The Heron Folds the Map

The heron folds her paper-thin map
lets the marsh breathe in her stillness
even the wind holds its tongue for her

The sky hums with invitations unanswered
branch, rooftop, reedbed, ridge
each one a door she's not yet ready to walk through

She dreams in thermals and cloud seams
knowing rest is its own migration
while the marsh shields her whereabouts

Winter's Mirror

I.

At the sill of morning, a sparrow
tests the air with one foot lifted
snow holding its breath
every doorway pretends finality
yet the light keeps saying *enter*
in a language learned by wings

II.

The same sparrow, later
remembers the cold by its name
feathers have learned
that crossing out and crossing back
are the same verb
conjugated by weather

III.

A cardinal stitches red into the cold
needle flashing, thread unseen
what we call silence is only
the room birds leave for song
to arrive without knocking
already inside the house

IV.

A crow revises the sky, black line
drawn and redrawn over frost
nothing wasted —
not the failed flight
not the pause midair
where doubt learns how to balance

V.

At the sill of evening, a sparrow
lifts the same foot, snow breathing
the door is still a door —
the light still says enter —
this time, the threshold answers back
with wings

Again: The Open Field
January – April 2026

The Plain

The hill is behind me,
but its shadow walks beside.

The field opens its palms,
and I see how much was waiting —
roots whispering, *We kept your place.*

I lay my papers on the ground.
The wind does not take them.
It reads.

All around me, the ordinary glows —
the stone, the stalk, the smallest seed —
as if they, too, remember the climb.

No trumpets, no gate.
Just the plain,
receiving my bare feet.

The Ones Who Watch the Sky

At first light, an eagle rises unseen,
her wings reading thermals like scripture
Below, the valley fills with watchers —
some whisper she's still climbing
some pretend they never saw her go

The eagle never calls down to explain
never breaks the purpose of her flight
she circles higher until clouds open their palms

At that height, the air thins to clarity
work becomes wind
silence becomes song

Far beneath, the watchers squint
awed by what they see

blinded by proof

Breathe Soft, Aurora

I.

Morning leaned on my shoulder
like it knew my name
coffee cooled in the pause
of everything I've been carrying

I thought I was behind
somehow fallen off the map
but the road kept answering
with footprints looking back

II.

There are ledgers in my bones now
ink I never meant to keep
clocks still turning under skin
guarding time instead of sleep

What I built did not announce itself
no bells, no ribbon in the air
just doors that open quietly
while I stood listening there

III.

Even the weary have a light
it flickers, but it stays
I can feel the ground beneath me
holding all my yesterdays

So I rest inside the distance
I once begged the sky to send
and call it by its truest name:
the road that does not end

Author's Note

The Hand Extended

A poem is a hand extended,
ink still warm from the passage

What I could not say
in real time I am writing now —
clean, intact,
after the first door opened

But a hand knows
when it is met in full

When I extend it now
it will not be empty —

it will hold the map
of how I found a way through

The Hand Extended began as a promise written in the middle of the Grammy ® consideration period — a moment when I had vowed I would document the journey in real time, but couldn't. I was simply trying to survive it. The social media updates stopped and the editorials never came. What arrived instead were poems.

The Grammy ® Submission Guide is the fulfillment of that promise — written from the other side, with steadier hands. It was what my past self needed: accurate information for the independent artist walking the uncertain path of submitting work for consideration by fellow recording professionals. Here it is, passed carefully from my hand to yours.

https://scriptaluna.press/grammy-submission-guide

For Jon Phipps — from the beginning

So let the poem be slow to rise
let no bright bell disturb its pace
a single gaze, another poet's eyes —
he saw it, pressed his thumb,
kept rocking on the porch
and that was more than most

Acknowledgments

This book was written in the hours before I learned how to defend my own voice without losing faith.

Katherine May faithfully supported the years behind this work. Though invisible on the page, her contributions were emotionally immense.

For the ones who carried the relay: John Pineiro made the first call. Tamanie Dove answered it without hesitation. Daniel Fisher spent two and a half hours making sure it was filed correctly. Ryan Schmidt, Esq. is a music lawyer who knows what it costs to make something. His contracts read like protection.

To my dogs, Rosa Barks and Barkin' Luther King, who kept me company through every late night and never once asked me to explain myself, I'm grateful.

To my family, in Atlanta and around the world, who don't think they like poetry, and yet have been speaking it to me all along.

Jon Phipps was my first writing partner — not collaborative, but parallel. We wrote side by side on allpoetry.com. He is the poet of the mountains in "Tea Leaves Brewing."

Amanda Dzimianski's editorial gift was the ability to identify the manuscript's true center of gravity from the outside. This book would not have found its clarity without her.

Like the women who carried their books of hours into marriages and across borders, I carried this one through an ordeal. It is offered now, in the same spirit — privately made, handed forward.

About the Author

Silvia Passiflora is a Southern Gothic Folk poet-songwriter and Grammy®-considered artist who guides listeners with an ukulele, banjo, and spoken word, offering safe passage past life's cliffhangers. Her 2025 releases, alongside the single "Pokeberry Letter" (Grammy®-considered for Best American Roots Song), travel the long road between beauty and grief.

Born in the Philippines and carried to Hawaii's shores, Passiflora grew up among gardens and kitchens, learning patience, craft, and the discipline of observation. A classically trained chef, certified sommelier, master gardener, and meticulous keeper of metadata, she cherishes the cultivation of each discipline like heirloom seeds.

With nearly two thousand poems and an expanding body of poetic screenplays, including the serialized Midnight Fields project, her work moves seamlessly between page and performance.

Traveling across Atlanta, Charleston, and Nashville, her performances capture the electricity between a story and the crowd leaning in to listen.

Also by Silvia Passiflora

Poetry In Flagrante

The complete and ongoing body of work — poems written
in real time, available at silviapassiflora.com

Writing under the moon.

Scriptaluna Press · Atlanta, Georgia

Set in Caladea · Printed in the United States of America